T0321421

TRANZ

TRANZ

Spencer Williams

Four Way Books
Tribeca

Library of Congress Cataloging-in-Publication Data

Names: Williams, Spencer, 1995- author.
Title: Tranz / Spencer Williams.
Other titles: Tranz (Compilation)
Description: New York : Four Way Books, 2024.
Identifiers: LCCN 2024000675 (print) | LCCN 2024000676 (ebook) | ISBN
9781961897168 (trade paperback) | ISBN 9781961897175 (epub)
Subjects: LCGFT: Poetry.
Classification: LCC PS3623.I56357 T73 2024 (print) | LCC PS3623.I56357
(ebook) | DDC 811/.6--dc23/eng/20240122
LC record available at https://lccn.loc.gov/2024000675
LC ebook record available at https://lccn.loc.gov/2024000676

This book is manufactured in the United States of America and printed on
acid-free paper.

Four Way Books is a not-for-profit literary press. We are grateful for the assistance
we receive from individual donors, public arts agencies, and private foundations
and the New York State Council on the Arts, a state agency.

We are a proud member of the Community of Literary Magazines and Presses.

Contents

sex dream about jesus

after Cameron Awkward-Rich

i'm pissed because i love the man and this is the same as being reminded the world is a disintegrating mess of oil and balding overlords. trees with red centers cut into books with terrible politics. so it remains imperative i kill the vibe he's on. i'm not the kind of girl who cares about dirty laundry. i'm not some final girl with a death wish and a septum ring. i want the man who cares about wanting. i want the man that doesn't make me boil with indifference. he was there and so i loved him. embarrassing no? i want the man to wrestle my misfortune of having been born, to tame it and make it call him "daddy." i want sex like a cis girl on coke wants water. i drink soda at midnight just to sit up with him for longer. i'm foolish for wanting what is commonly sinister. his podcast is the same thing as a threat. i'm a tranz sex monster. i touch about him in public restrooms as praxis. you take me, i take you. what i love about him is that he can't reach the top shelf but refuses to bottom. i like the man's ambition beyond his grasp. i love him like i'm about to never pray again. you know what i mean? i edge over the block button. i edge over my pillow. he knows i'm dying by the minute. that six months in on hrt has made my sperm devoid of childhood. for him, i undress my bank account and slap its bare ass. love him like only a woman like me can love: meaning, if i die tomorrow, he did it. your honor, it was him. the life of a trans girl is tragic in his imagination.

but i want him like the reaper wants takeout. i want him like a small cousin wants your old iphone six. in the story of our love, the one our kids will learn, he met me on the porch of a nuclear test site and ravaged the unsqueezable plastic of my tits, ass, and cantankerous pussy. i'm not a romantic in the romantic era sense. there's no consumptive fantasy which motivates my hunger. i'm romantic in that i believe in fucking up a lawn chair. head game like a mantis. what teeth i have. i gave up politics for his wicked mouth. i'm cruel and ditzy, a lollipop with hair. in bed, he puts one hand on my girldick and the other on the heat of my scabbing heart.

A body is not a prologue, and its story can be written at will.

—Sasha Geffen

tranzgender statement of purpose

it's like   we get it:

the index of bruises
i've incurred as tranz

could constitute their own cartography.

       in any context where i'm seen

i'm less woman than a womb
inside a jar, but we'll end there

       and start again:

in this new state we call safe
i'm fucking ur husband on the balcony
and it's tits-free-to-the-air kind of romantic.

beyond us

       fir trees stand erect in the yard

       ur bratty dog dry humps the white leg
       of a plastic patio chair

the breeze mutters *disgusting*

so we agree
there's nothing else to do
but step back indoors.
but first, he wants to smoke.

(men always stall when on the edge of error)

i say fine. i'll go piss and make the bed warm.

like i've won something,
i open the door behind us
leading into ur room
and let me all
the way inside.

ode to panic

ur tranz panic is what it is

but i have titties now   mom mutters *shit*

when she forgets   but it's ok.

a pronoun is collapsing   infrastructure anyways

on tik tok u can be   a blade   of grass

or a teapot   and i want to be   nothing

if not   forgettable.   i still have   friends

who can't fathom   why i don't want

to hear their thoughts   on gr8   trans art

the process of simply standing   in a room

with no bra.   simply repeating

oneself into a rhythm   i lather in tranz

let u wash it off   no girl wants to be tranz-passing tho

so many are

yes   this pleases me

for better or worse   panic is   a continuous loop

i want to spectate   from a distance.   my titties say *out*

they're mine   i watered them.

watched them   take to the sun   like a cat wanting

whatever side of the door   u neglect

i am not dangerous   until i'm made in the mouth

of someone who fears me   mom says *sorry* on the phone

the guilty resonance   burns

like a wet willy   from god

my pronouns r mud   in my hands

i move   to my legs   then move in between them

trans art is a question

the answer is always.   yes i have

friends who love me for having been   their first

panic.   a paradox   u won't hear loudly enough

i can't fear u less   until u fear me less—

yes, the dream of babies is

a silly dream.

in the womb, tequila
spoils the cranium

and stalls adulthood. my
ability to cope is a hole

where my birth
mother sits. our family

tree is
a drowning child

gasping towards
a pock of light

too distant to be useful.
the goal has always been

to be moderate, a good
woman preserved

by limitation. no longer do i
drink to bed, hoarding bottles

for the dull shine of aesthetics.
though at times, i'm still haunted.

i dream

another silly dream. i sit
in the center of an empty room,

encircled by glasses. one by one,
i lift empty cylinders and chew

through them, watching the blood
in my mouth water the floor.

a fountain. i don't stop leaking
color where at first there was none.

god is a suspect male musician

in the garage of my youth, i scooped cat shit into plastic bags
while singing britney.

kids i knew smoked weed in parking lots
and got kicked out of "hairspray."

i am still envious of the christian girls who called me "sissy,"
the horse-haired blondes who gave me

my first taste of hell. i am still envious of brad, who kicked
my ass behind a 7/11 dumpster and was the first man

to get me hard. my first medal was for memorizing hymns.
sometimes, i tried so hard to be good i felt empty.

sometimes, being good is the same as being ruthless.
i learned this at camp. i learned lots of things at camp,

like how every christian rock song sounds a little gay.
or like how "faggot" is a title you don't have to work for

if you smile enough. around the fire, twenty-year-old
counselors strummed like virgin sirens.

not once did i ask anyone to die for me, but there i was,
ready to donate my 4 commissary dollars to the imperial

project of missionary aid. my first high was courtesy of a tube
sock, some glue, and a ceiling fan.

kids my age lit fires in the sinks of their high school bathrooms.
all i wanted back then was to dye my hair.

all i wanted was to learn kelly clarkson songs on bass.
my brother tried to get me into the cure. i said fuck that.

ashlee simpson. kids i grew up with died as kids. in college, i
stood awkward at house shows with a photo of my sister

in my pocket. none of my jeans were skinny when it
mattered. someone told me i should relax more

and even now i agree. to this day, i am envious of STEM
majors who can sing. to this day, i want to universally

cancel improv. when i first left cali, i prayed on the top loft
of my dorm room every night for three months.

then, my first roommate stepped in front of a moving car.
my second high was courtesy of a hand mirror, a basement,

and an antique spoon. kids i grew up with fist-fought
over holographic trading cards. kids i grew up with

weren't queer where i could feel it. my first kiss
was an assault. my second concert was one direction.

once, i believed in god so hard,
u couldn't tell me shit about lonely.

birth mother

i find her while roaming on
the internet at 3am.

i don't
send message,
though i hover.
when i was born
again,

meaning twice,
my heart stopped.

tequila blood. mouth
latched to
the flesh of a lime.

i miss
my birth
mother

but she might've killed me,
birth mother.

when i threw
that sloppy fist

towards
the face of a
stranger,

was that you?

that night
i used one hand
to sweep

glass into
the other, i
tried speaking
through

the water in
my lungs. *silly
bitch,* i spewed.

who was i
talking to?

flashlight in
hand, i walked
to the woods

and kicked my
shoes beneath
a tree. i
unbuttoned

my shirt,
my shorts, walked
over mud in briefs,
bobbing light

        from branch to branch.

                birth mother.

                i thought i saw
                    you there
                in the clearing.

                    my one
                    good eye

running over

the crown of
a doe, her nose

pressed cold
against
the earth.

you. did not
startle, even
as i stood

so close
and fearful.
slowly, you
lifted

and caught
me in a glare.
there was
nothing else.

i collected

my clothes,

brushed
the dirt
from my feet.

doctors hate her **says the internet ad**

hello.

i tossed epsom salt in my bath and pretended
to heal something.

ate fries
said *vegetable*.

at the dawn of a new millennium, i stopped circusing
for healthcare, so if i die it's because i demanded

the good time i was owed. the best barebacks happen
in church pews. god used to be inside of me

until i made him pull out.

the story goes i hated men and then, when i was born,
i had a reason to. in a utopia trans girls get paid for nothing

but their presence.
my dad is 84.

i can't imagine
who i'll be when he is gone,

either a harlot or a daughter
still desperate for a name. can u believe

my disgust over trans this and trans that
stopped me from getting fucked?

if u hate me, thank u
for thinking of me.

thank u for allowing me to be here
despite u.

look.
i won't be shamed for my ambitions.

like how i want the earth on one knee
so when i spit down from space,

america can dutifully open
wide and catch, swallow.

revising the danish girl

1.

true story: i went for a walk.

the sun was hidden by the dark

    flank of a cloud, but the shine bled through,

barely grazing the water. a brush of pink

    perverting the tranquil white of a sheet.

there were ducks with their feet tucked in, pushed

by gentle breeze beneath the bridge. it took forty minutes

    to walk home, and in that time i counted fifteen

blossoms, four carriages, and thirty-one pairs of eyes

unblinking.

sometimes, a woman is a man in how she stares.

everywhere i go, i am made of

some kind of sun.

2.

look,

this city is one long telephone wire

weaving in and out of each brick,

a language you can learn.

each bell toll, a bit of gossip.

on a bridge after rain, i bent down to face the water.

what i saw there

shocked me

with a joy so disruptive,

it surged at the toes and ended where all things end:

the tongue.

3.

a girlish thought:

when i pressed my center with one

hand, i could

almost feel the kicking there, the vase of me pleading

to be filled.

i confess: there is not a color to rival how it feels

to be so woman.

no canvas wide enough to capture the landscape it inspires:

dainty, fleshing hills,   swollen clouds of milk,

a crowd of poppies

gathering like pigeons over bread, and above,

                    that smear of sky, two fingers tracing

                    the jaw of my lover, down to her

crossed feet.

4.

i believe, at the end of the world,

        i will need only the empty stomach

of a cathedral, its barren echo,

        the woman i will marry

and the woman i have named.

i believe i will be old

when i die,

    and when i die

    my love will hold—

    no—keep
        like a door held
        open.

the pact

little ghost, you. an ashtray
pluming in the dark.
up through morning,
i nodded to the branches
scratching at my window.   grief, like
a flutter of wings on the sill.   a coo.
it startled me, you know.   the sun.
i'm no good in shadow, am prone
to drinking heavy. a mob of one.   detached,
with a gun to my head, i can
speak only in apology. nowhere now,
you're missing my best work yet,
these years of metabolic highs and lows.

o departed,
yesterday there was a cat in the yard   eating snow.
                                                                And suddenly:
                                                                        this,

the limbs of a poem moving recklessly.
love, like a spreading bruise. from my hip

to the nape of my neck,   a sorry excuse for a map.
it still troubles me,

that thought: where you
                                                          went,

i could've gone, if i wanted.
but i didn't. what i desired instead
was so simple it hurt. to be. to have been   a better house
around you. to know i was   not capable of
                                                          worse.

origin

sections to be read in the mirror
after torrin a. greathouse

The first thing you lose when you waver in and out is an anchor. The image of your birth mother's face looms above you, then fades as you're ushered in. The shape of her lips— what was that again? There is no such thing as color. Nurses whiz by in a blur of off-white. You manifest inside a pale room with a table to lay on and a desk littered with empty syringes. Your mother's eyes empty over you, two cavernous gaps. You're barely there, so it's hard to determine why she's there too. You wonder what she'd say if she could see you now, in your delirium, vomit birthmarked at the side of your mouth.

anchor   The first

      looms   birth mother

            again There is

    inside   a blur

delirium   You

    of you

You wonder if she'd turn away. Roll her eyes. She wouldn't cry. Allow yourself to consider this: the stoicism you project helps ease your guilt. In your half-conscious frolicking between there and not, you don't want her to see you, don't want to confirm the thing you pretend is something else, even when you call adoptive mother to explain a $700 bill you can't afford to pay, and a part of you erodes when she picks up.

the   allow

ease

you don't want

pretend   don't

a part of you

a part of you   a part of you

You forget mothers, perhaps on purpose, and whatever phase of moon her mouth makes when you say something crass— something about the good sex you wish you were having, or the bad sex that was done to you, without you, as you lay there in blackout, blood drying in your nostril like a sunswept creek.

her   perhaps

               you   mouth makes

                you

    you   you   you

       like a creek

The second wave of things lost includes the living. You stare
across the room at the doctor and see not the lines in his face,
but the motion of his skull, how his jawbones clack together
to mimic the sounds of talking. Through his white coat,
you locate the heart, a smallish prune unbeating through
his naked rib. You turn your head, see the window. Squint
and see no sky. No moon. Just pitch. On your wrist, the last
bright thing you have left to tear.

    You

    mimic

  the heart, a smallish

             window. You squint and see

      you have left

This will not be the last time you're forced to lie still in this room. You do not know this, but maybe, in the click of your bones, you do. When you're discharged the next day, you make note of all the empty rooms you pass as you leave. You feel queasy, lungs wearing last night's dress of dark mineral.

You think, I'm good.

the

bones

all the empty   discharge

wear   you

good.

You find it hard to be moderate. Everything is framed two ways: obsession or casual disdain. Your teenage self mocks you in the bathroom, flipping you off. You are two separate people now anyways. She frowns at your sentences. Your friend asks *should we do coke* and the answer is obviously yes. You admire the ordinariness of this question as if it were a loose branch framed in a window. You think ordinary suits you. There's no blood to mop up after. No chipped tooth to correct. You do a line, then fall back into the sofa. Comfortable. Imagine yourself casual, not casualty. The line could not be thinner. You snort that too and now your head hurts a little. In the morning, it'll feel like a hangover caught flame. No matter. You'll drink water. Attack the day. Rinse. Repeat.

Everything is casual

You mock you

You people You

sentences

the casual

you

There's no

Comfortable.

thinner. you

little. you

You Attack Repeat.

An ending: a friend catches you fingering your name into a fresh patch of vomit. As if in a dream, you look up to the sound of his voice, a reverberating mess of language. The ceiling spins above you. Two men—you think they're men—rush in and disappear you. The routine repeats, as if someone outside of you has hit rewind, wound back the tape to your initial visit, forced you to watch. First, you, carried in on a tray like an expensive meal. Second, the glass of rock, which hollows you.

An ending: you finger you   into

you   vomit.

language.   a

you.

repeat

you

"Do you have anyone to call?" someone asks.

"No," you say. You will walk home with another wristband.

"Do you have anyone that can come pick you up?"

"No, but I'll see you again in a few weeks," you joke.

"Next time is police," someone says,
but you pretend you don't hear.
You're trying not to giggle.

you have

No   say. You   walk   with

anyone that can

see you

you   someone says, but

don't hear.

You take time. You smoke weed, which is fine. When you go
to acquire hormones at a women's clinic in Iowa City, you fill
out a questionnaire about medical history. You consider lying.
For the first time in a while, you require a drug you actually
need. Ok. So you lie when the questionnaire asks "suicide?",
and your brain says "this is addict behavior." You say you
know, but this is different. Capital "M" Medical. You can't
remember a time when you didn't feel anxious.

You

a   acquire

history. You consider

the

addict behavior.

a

you didn't feel   time

At the clinic, the things you remember arrive in bursts. The first line on the table of a party you were dragged to. The first pipe handed off in the back of a pool hall. First hot spoon. The first time your face broke out with oozing landmarks. For a while, these are the things you touch to avoid the other things. But they all begin to slow drip into your day, like the first rape, when you woke in a room at a party. How at first you thought you'd lost your pants, then tried to stand, and knew. The warm red wet on the sheet that wasn't yours.

arrive in bursts   you

The pipe   the table

landmarks   the

you touch

The rape

lost   another

you

You get your pills in the end (another ending). You grow a new body to forget the old one, but the old one persists. You leave mid-sentence. Briefly forget the names of close friends. Simple objects. You get worried, google symptoms. Can't find conclusive evidence to suggest memory is one of the things you can lose. You elongate the worry nonetheless. You catch yourself blanking while you teach class, stammering over words that suddenly don't make sense in your mouth. The room goes white and then you're back. Time is up. Your students depart and you lag behind, wiping the blackboard. The notes on symbol, metaphor. You look at your work, the chalky leftover ash. You smear the contents. You flip the lights. You leave the room.

a worg uoY .(   ) bne   uoY

uoY   ybod

                    forget

Can't find   uoY

                    memory

          uoY   uoY esol   uoY

                    uoY   blank

                    don't make sense.

                              you

depart   you   clean.

You

light   the room.

I am not what I am. I am what I do with my hands.

—Louise Bourgeois

laramie

miraculously / i grew / am grown / woman /
tranny whore / faggot / it doesn't matter / what geography

makes of the word / an erasure / is only a poem
if a body is unearthed / it matters then / that all

my stories / eat like worms / drown in rain /
repeat in anger / faggot of the flesh / faggot

on the porch / it doesn't matter / where
i once existed / or exist / if it is written

when i was young / my parents
drove us through laramie /

and as a child / i knew not one / smear of history /
least of all / a faggot's / but in the car / dad cut

the sound / of a cd skipping / until /
just the three of us / me / my mom

and him / all quiet / a blur of town /
a ghost / or a gasp / framed by window /

faggot in the blood / faggot in the field /
i didn't know / the middle of nowhere

is also a place / people live / and die in /
but i've been there / intimately /

miraculously / am grown / perhaps in
the only time / i can be / a gust / if that /

or / anywhere i choose / just barely.

postcard from dover, new hampshire, 2009

in a smog of weed
noa falls over on the carpet
near the closet, where inside

you are changing into one of her mom's
leftover nightgowns, tacky with dust.
your high is a somersault, brain

like a radio mid-storm. pull away
from the door and its taped-up idols,
from little sisters begging for passwords in.

you emerge from the closet not fully formed
but as a secret unclenched in the mouth
of want. "daughter" is still a noun

you keep, unconcerned, like a mint
in your pocket. noa says "you look hot"
and this matters for reasons you can't name yet.

pull away from her bed, its promise of chill.
from the dog in the yard barking as insects spark up,
then fade, like tension. pass it back. the bad stash

rolled into courage. another mouthful
of hoarse laughter, another half-lit ceiling to gawk at.
better than a first kiss. and the dress upon you now,

not yours, but like any blazing fly
you seal inside a jar to watch,
a beacon.

poem about adrienne rich

on new year's eve i drink
my weight in tequila

watch the night transition
into migraine. then nothing

until dawn arrives too early
for what it is, birds

rattling the sill.
i call this a poem

angry at the taste of my mouth,

like a mouse crawled in there to die.
often, i mistake

my tongue for ruins.
memory is whatever

i want it to be. like how i'm sober
every day i'm not drinking. how

there's no proof i drank if i forgot.
this brings us to the book on my table.

sometimes i forget who i am,
but certain objects remind me.

i pull from the night's wreck

a joke i made: *drag name*
Adrienne Richard. not my best work.

maybe i drank too much because another poet
forgot, mid-convo, who i was suddenly. or what, as in,

what kind of faggot. often, i find myself
in a state of acute desperation. i'll read yet
another epigraph,

another epigraph, another, and wonder
what it's worth to ruin a party. *tell me,*

i beg
in my brain, where all my begging

works. *how her poems*
speak to u. so i can tell u the name

of a sister who is not here
to sister anymore. often, i think about

                              what else is commonly
forgotten.
we keep a poet's

        mind and work and think them
        beautiful and separate. but any trans will tell u.

dirt is dirt before it's a metaphor
for tranny. and so, in this poem

i dig out "woman," however she's defined,
and allow her entry into my

                              language.   here,
                              in a poem,

every woman
is allowed dominion.

and just like that, i remember
how done i was pretending

art matters
when the cost

is who we are. i said this
to a man who said

that's not how art works.
the book on my desk

is half-read. sometimes, in order to read,
i have to loathe. i have to loathe in order

to advance beyond loathing.
all this, for a book, a woman who

is dead, and those who keep putting
her bones on the table. who keep telling me

to look. ok. i've looked.
i've looked, ok. and now
i'm done with looking.

one dose of anxiety meds later

friend died. cat died. i finally took a breath and nothing
changed except i'm not sucking off men who make beats

with their roommates, am sturdy in my refusal to eat ass
for anything less than an "i love u" text.

in the fleeting months of professional plant nursing,
i started saying "love" to mom again, stopped cringing

inside hugs that were earnest. i didn't get murdered and this
doesn't have to be the moral even as it remains the goal,

since after years of totally bro'ing it
i sold out for a pair of a-cup tits and a never-ending

spectacle of hatred. can u believe i still have the capacity for
love in the face of men and youtube skincare regiments?

that i still love horniness disguised as a death threat
in my inbox? when all else fails, love lingers like a bullet

on the table. done with stalling, i'm placing a bounty
on my clit so at last she can be found.

have u seen her? on the milk carton. on the public access television. everywhere i go i am there so brutally.

i say i am tranz and

there must be no death quite like the birth
of a woman. mother stands from the table
at the cold stone creamery.

what i've said: i am no one.

what i meant to say: i have abandoned nothing.

isn't it funny how the absence
of a man still swallows the room?

if i can be frank about language

inside the "i" there is a world i can offer
no visitor. the rooms are chilly
but they are mine and i stand in them,
watching wheels snap off the carriage mother
pulls in her head.

where have i gone.
when did i leave. why did i drag

what god had given me out back
to skin.

                        mother.

i take pity on ghosts.

how they dangle like loose web and catch
between the hand. i promise

                        i only wanted
the *him*
of me
gone,

pulled from my language
as if hair from a drain.

i heard   in the gap
        my voice.

now mother.

what past are you staring at.

> i already know
> there is no body
> behind me.

this night too will end
> after Against Me!'s album *Transgender Dysphoria Blues*

laura
 when i first
    listened to your record
       i rode home
          on the back
    of a broom
          shouting out for a reason
          not to strip
buck naked in the street
          right then
       and there—suddenly
          every inch of wrong my body
          was told
          to shelter
       shriveled
                against the tremor
             of that gruesome
                   sound

                i flung with glee
          beneath a tire
                flashed my tits
          at ripple waves
             sun-cast

upon the granite
        and that was
      the first
       sundown i howled
      through the navel
       of an lp towards
    a barren sky
     the first evening
i sought to baptize the tatter
   of every dress i owned
            in cum

i clawed my chest
       cut curling hair
         down to the skull
snuck out the back door
     and into that record
repeating the faggot in me
   unable to catch
her breathe   so
      thank god for that
gym membership
all that grace
and summer sick

turned beauty   i swear
that record was
the first time i came
of age again
gripping
the fresh kill
of a dead name   in my jaw

laura
i was there
feet rank,
delicious
from moshing

out towards the rafters
of an empty church
the graffiti wall
next to the railway
the third floor of a hotel
hallway
red-orange like
the shining
the first film i saw
with a crush

before
he took me
to his bedroom
with the intention
of meat
then pleasure

laura
i could not
name
what i was then
or how i wanted
him
to prepare me
so i sat
on the floor
and begged
for water
turned
and saw
outstretched
his cock
an angry
flex

said *suck*
said *now*
said *boy*
bitch
became so
bitch of me
to run home
though i did   run crying
track two
throbbing like a kiss
in my ear
i guess   better to be
alive bitch
than dead bitch
yes   better to be
alive—

laura
for a time
i performed
altar boy duties at
st. matthew's episcopalian
back when I thought   only

gay thoughts   not
        woman thoughts
    the proof
   that god blessed
my transgender heart
  is how   when he walked me
   from the bird bath
my family half-
  drowned me in
       i did not burst
   into hellfire

  laura
it's true
 i believe god
 so loved
this earth he made
you pluck dead petals
  from my tongue
  and drop them onto
  the dark curve
   of an empty road
  and sure   it's all dramatically
  contrived to call

a record   rehabilitation
but i can't lie   say
                    i haven't found a cure
                                for body
lodged in the gutter muck
                    of a punk song before

            with the headbang collision
of a plastered bedroom wall
                    that i haven't
            found my way back
    to limbs i keep
                    ghosting
                    because a singer cried
with you   with you
            and maybe meant
with me
so then   the trial becomes
                    how to un-ugly
        this non-passing life
how to restructure   the bones
                    in their frame
            i mean—
        i look

in the mirror
        once a day
      glimpse
  this wretched
surface
    know   there is no handy
          denial no
    fantasy football crowd
        tilting me towards
            heaven
              on a great mass
              of shoulders

              laura   my god
          how i want
            this dick
              to be
              meaningless
                  to have it be
            a twisted branch
                  so close
                  to snapping
                everyone is
              scared to cross

beneath it

laura   once
i listened to
that record
on a walk home
from the park
when a group
of boys   my age
circle-   jerked
my   fear into
the center   of their hands
made me
lick
each palm   clean
of my own
red gloss

laura   please
if i could define
my dysphoria to you
it would be
a constant desire
to be   attractive

and already dead
at the same time
to have the shit
kicked out of me
as fetish
for a minute

could you imagine
a lover like that
toothpicking gore
from my teeth in
the afterplay
of torture
yes   on the worst days
this is what i tell
myself i want
like how
he won't
kill me
if he gets the chance
to pretend he did

laura
i think

if i want anything
it's considerable
practice at cheating
death or else
a fair shot
at filling my
grave with
dead names
dead friends

dead skin
dead reasons not
to strip my face clean
from the bone
and grow back
something legible
woman is not
a destination for me
cuz i've been living
inside one for some
time now
incubating in glorious
arrival

laura

when the lights
          cut out
     i am touching myself
a future
          without curdled blood
                    touching
          another person
               with the feral heat
          of an untamed beast
               i mean
               is it so impossible
     for us to be unremarkable
               in how we're desired
                    just once
     i'd like to be couched in
               by pillows
          in a room with   familiar
warmth not
          quenching for
tranz sacrifice

laura
is there any
          room left   in me

to hope
i won't be doomed   forever
some sweat-
slicked fever
cascading off
a stranger's brow
that true love
will find me
like that record did
coursing down
my legs
the night i pondered
leaping
into god's view
through the roof
of a passing
honda civic

laura
i mean to say that once
there was
a voice   that pulled me
backwards
from condolence

that once i listened
to that closing track
four times
until the moon
blacked out
into grimace

laura
i think
i can take

this life

as a stiff

drink
learn how

to love

whatever dark

the sky brings

when the sun

won't take

dance to

whatever hell

they have left

to show me

whatever heaven

i can't touch

with both hands

if this

is all i get

laura yes

i'm going to

kiss each scab

where the light

breaks through

and marks me

just a little

just a little

which came first, my fear of men or ibs

hard to say truly   but the social experiment
that is america
has birthed men who'll tell you

frogs are gay

something in the chemicals

or maybe frogs just like it
to hurt

when i was seventeen
i stayed with a mennonite family

and survived on the multiplicities
of a potato   what i learned was
horse shit can be used to
heat a home
and in a poem i can say *kill
all men*

and mean anything

the structure
or a hole   i fuck to sleep

in america
what tastes good is usually corn
what sounds like korn is usually confederate
                                    my
                whole life has been a series
                of men asking
                me to confirm
they are good for
what they are   my advice is always

"transition"

    i am tired of being   a day priest
    i am tired of shitting too fast
    after eating   once i went home with a man
                    i'll do anything once

a man walks into a bar
and shoots my people
                        a man walks into a bar
and orders peanuts   a man walks into a bar
and becomes   president

i want to know why all men sneeze like they're made of tnt

i want to know why   my ass holds
a grudge

     in a poem i can leave the body
     anywhere

   i can lose twenty pounds

           and hate crime u
           back—

**in sweden, the first womb-transplant reveals a baby boy,
but i am still trans and this is still a personal fiction**

though the contemporary science of uterus transplants
is past the stage in the hypothesis where rats are key performers,
i like to imagine them bustling about
in trench coats, fat tails flickering against a backdrop
of sheer white.

i'm at an age when normally i'd be asked
about the future. if i have a maternal aspiration
and *why don't* i if i don't?

in the bath, i close my eyes
and talk to you, or me, as a mother talks in her sleep,
then wakes, imagining the worst has happened.

around her, a quiet which suggests a lack of liveliness,
a margin for error suddenly crossed. naked in suds,
i submerge and try to feel my way back. i reach out
and tell her that we're fine. the two of us,

half-madonna and child, still here amongst the living.
from makeshift womb to back again,
it doesn't matter how cruelly i receive the world.
the fact is simple. when i rise, i am clean.

tranz

the story goes   i saw
my face   once   in the reflection of a screen
and thought wow   my face   is not
   what my face is

the joke is that   every tranz girl
            named heather or something
               cottage-y
            goes to grad school
      to play harp   neg chasers   cop surgeries

   but honestly
i don't care about some app-guy's amorousness
            i am still my most valid
   talking shit about strangers
on ur iphone hotspot   accustomed to grief
   i participate in every game of hangman
            eat   annie's mac and cheese
straight from the pot   over the clothes
         of my dead friends

u know   just tranz shit   i don't internalize
      it already takes   a certain kind
of muscle to speak   to be heard

on any given day   my pronouns are   kettle/bell/s
                              rise/and/grind

                                                  my/neck/my/back
                    and look
        it's my own dumb luck   that i'm tranz at a time
when the internet exists   now i'm nothing without
fetish   idk   it's not my fault   every man in my dms
wants a lick   of glory   hole
          that in every tranz poem
            there's   a broken foal   bucking to climax
                              over   yellowing grass
      a horse bleeding out
upon the daisies   the blurry dick pic
      of a mare
                        in the economy of tranz
            a poem   is the same thing as a handout
and each horse is obviously the fag
    i ride off on
                    every page
see me   half teeth   half monstrous schlong
                                            see me

at twenty-six i'm getting better at distilling my rage

a fear of being judged is the two-hundred-and-seventh bone
in the body and no surgery can shave it down or cut it out.

my father still calls me son, but with a different tone than before,
as when i accomplish a goal:

"i'm proud of you *son*"

like he might sense i'm about to leave and wants to lure me
back without the theatre of forgiveness.

would it kill someone to know

i'm not any less of a wound now,
more accurately a slight bruise, not purple or foreboding

but there, creeping under the sleeve
like a birthmark only a lover would notice.

after years of cold turkey, i've turned the blinkers on
and it's amazing what i can see, but also what i couldn't

on the mend, like my own hands and what hurts they made.
how april fools i was pretending i could stand

without a wall, or eat without a hunger.

bruce springsteen's *Nebraska* was the last noise i conked out
to five summers ago, and now the album plays like

the kind of memory u keep when u don't want all the parts
but a handful justify the rest so you make do.

a secret is that everyone wants to suffer
to survive. to say they've been to hell and back and learned

the lessons. but there are none in a place called hell.
on the verge of dying, i felt the body fail. there was

nothing i could do.

i didn't push beyond that failure, and so it stuck to me
and i drag it—now— to the cvs, to a place called home

and to the bus. to my parents' house. to a lover's
bed and out of it towards the bathroom and also

to the kitchen for water. i made peace with my face.
i look good in a desperate light.

humbled, like a moth is humbled by its god.

the one we made to better see
the road at night.

if ur gonna be transphobic at least be funny

the year is 1995 and i am born into the livestream,
    a particle of man continuously
clicking through breasts
      of all shapes in the banner. click me
       says angelbabyxoxo i'm in ur area etc;
and the typeface sticks like a good kind of threat

        because in 2021 all i can think of
          when asked to flagellate
          over some violent
           hypothetical is
         yeah, i'm in ur area
           when someone clicks
       just to tell me i'm trans
  which i am
   which i was even when the word
     was confounding   come get me then
           come do it
       come on now
 i'm in ur area.
      it's actually quite
simple: first i was born, then
     things got boring.
         when i say i'm "online"

i mean that everyone i've never met
                wants me to know they're disgusted
        by the possibility of my cock   as if
            i told them to sit there and imagine it
                my loathing staff   my unbearable
pansy rope wrapped viciously around their necks
                                    if it mattered
                                    i would say i'm no
                                    longer
                interested in the forum's
        vocabulary   that i've
                    evolved past the need
            for fucking anyways
                        having replaced my libido
        with a lust for conservationism
that i've retired to the mountains
                    of a national park
                        where you can find me explicitly
        not jerking off the grizzly bear
                but stroking its coarse fur   feeding
                        the beast berries and kibble
from the meat
    of my open hand.
like any predator

the anglosphere has filthy claws
                rupturing all the spending i did on this flesh,
my wiki of shovel-ready tits.
                              here's a thing i might be compared to
                    on the app if people had more vivid
          imaginations: an insect called
                          the japanese giant hornet
                    capable of killing 40 euro honeybees
                        in one minute.   if u know   u know
                                              on page-view
                        my tits are shamefully redacted. i speak
                    and 40 women
                                  stay pledging my death post-
                    webcast.
          "hornet honey" is what i call their bumbling noise
                    what i call each drop of childless sperm
what i call anonymous men who stay perpetually in my beeswax
bitch i'm over it
          the main stage   the podium
the this and that of personhood
                    just grab me a coffee coke
                            and let me
          smooth my brain out

things were so much simpler back
        when u
            cried watching boys don't cry
        and didn't know me
if ur gonna be transphobic
        can u not do it in front of my salad
        can u not do it with those bangs
          can u not do it with crumbs in ur beard
can u at least be hot
    can u at least make me feel bad   to know we won't be fucking

at the end of the day
    i'm just a woman   standing in front of the door
  of another woman's dms   begging her to take
        her own hate seriously
          if u have to ask
            how i'm doing
              u should know that i'm clicking
through an endless stream of cat vids for a piece of action
    another article where i am made   a study in cryptozoology
        at a certain point   u gotta admire the hustle
   of a ghost despite everyone's efforts   my voice on the evp
stays repeating
        fuck u fuck u   fuck u

rumination on a mother tongue

my girlbody tangled in yolk strings aside my sister. we
pull an embryonic distance between us through a thick
of reeds grey as assigned biology. our mother's womb
like hands digging out the fleshy core of pan de muerto.

in her we grew towards an outer rim of flimsy womb
so muted in pink as to be appear bashful by borders
the cruelty by which our faces would turn eventually
on the outside, invisible when facing each other.

near the edge, a plate leaps, then scatters. there are
weeds in the body thick with lust. the painter's hand
draws full reconfigurations: the body lines spiral, recede
against knots, the blood, the arteries, the umbilical as a
river, tubes indistinct like siblings with countries at war.

in water salt dissolves but keeps in the taste.
salt the border with mother's entrails.
leak cursive over both our names.

in a reoccurring dream, my sister and i are bulbous shapes stagnant and muddy, sheltering flies in dry creek beds. i believe it was my country who told me never give name to blood as though to share it. i kept a secret i didn't know i had—siblings i've never met rooting deep into my girth.

i thought if they are dead then i am buried too and the lot of us are plots of land floating like an archipelago beneath the ground. it is no use. If my blood sister's fingertips betray reflections of my own they are cursed to stain every surface with oil.

i outlived the salt burn of my birth but remain uncertain of the month my sister came, only that it happened, that it is as factual as the name i gave myself. if my blood sister's mouth resembles in shape my own, her tongue remains to me a stranger, meaning she must know this feeling too, can spell it out in ways i cannot translate.

when
my   adoptive
mother

traveled
to beijing   with
her brother

to bring
home his adopted
daughter

she
brought home   a
dish of red paste

for me
to   stamp my
name

my name became an imprint on every bedroom wall
a wound unbandaged and breathing.

fingers dragging softly
my name, my name
into the wall.

sister

the papers say the two of us

are not twins

even as i do not reject the idea

that we are, in some psychic way,

bridged by thread at the hipbone.

two, torn like a handful of loose

dark hair, two scabs browning

on both knees.

sister. where do

you reside?

when i pull hairs from my face...

is that you there in the wound?

is this you

you

threatening to bleed me?

in sleep i see birth
mother floating above
me bright pink and
naked as a prophecy.
she chokes down my
body until her mouth
floods with opposition.

on the night i was
conceived
mexico tangled birth
mother's hair into
canals of blood. seven
months later i entered
grave and

unpronounced.
how to name a dying
breath something other
than quick or facile.
how to trace the blood
back to a mother who
does not know i am no

longer what they first
called me.
how many ways to call
me sir
tranny

faggot

how many ways to deduce whether or not mother's
addiction inflicted upon me my penchant for the
dangerous, as in, how many men do we share between
us. how to carve birth mother out like a stone wedged
in my naval. how to say i am not her son, that i am
barely her daughter. how many ways to say daughter.

in a dream i address birth mother and ask her
to guess how many faces i see in the mirror
each day. ask her for the number of siblings that
know i am here. ask her to point me to the spot
where birth father touched her ferocious and
summoned me.

perhaps this is most accurately how i think of you dear sibling,
dear mother. in portrait. as borders struck down
by recognition. by this i mean i you best
by the homes that won't lay claim to me in full.

    when i close my eyes there is not one thing
    that owns me.

roots,

we are so many bodies between us

both here and not.

in chula vista i climb the hill towards my

house.

when i reach the top the border lifts me

in its gargantuan hand,

plays catch with my body.

feeds me

wholly to the sky.

at least he's happy

1.

when i was younger, my father would go camping every other weekend with some delinquent in need of the wilderness, or a church friend, or one of my stressed-out godfathers. my siblings and i were jealous—here was an intimacy we weren't allowed to encroach upon. we felt ourselves unwanted, reminders of a stable, boring home. but mostly, we felt bad for our mother and tried to nurse away her loneliness with noise. or i did. or i misinterpreted what it meant for a man to leave behind a woman in an empty home. didn't know it could also be construed as a blessing, a kind of peace. i bring this up because i've been thinking of the desert more and more—of the people that go missing in search of nirvana, or because they've been put under the spell cast by high temperatures. where the sound of nearby water is the threatened tail of a snake. meaning, my dad forgets we have a father we could lose. i want to attach a monitor to his belt loop, so that when he shouts for help, having lost his foot to the mouth of a rock bed, i'll come blazing down the highway in search of him, his pain, to mother back to civilization.

2.

how grand, the earth. it cares not for the nuclear. when one man goes missing, others follow, and then you have a commune surrounding the outline of their grief, the bone carried in a vulture's beak, suddenly dropped. what i'm saying is, reduced to symbol, a person can be anything that helps the rest move on. it's true that everyone becomes a deserter in their lives. mothers and fathers leave behind papers dictating property rights and monetary transfers. unpaid loans and dirty artifacts. children must take to archaeology. dust off the carbon, turn a home back into house. i suppose it is love which compels us to trash the plates we don't need, the paintings we find garish. i try not to think too hard about what has yet to arrive, but my brother says, at a certain age you start to count the visits. once or twice a year with eight years give or take, makes, at most, sixteen more times to say *i love you* in person. and then. and then what.

friendship, or i want to be where the men are

not in, but on the other side of the chain-link staring out at
the court as my friend rushes from the hoop to the three-

point line. ball in hand—then not—he becomes less than blur,
more a sturdy mass rounding the blacktop again,

again. the circle of his feet. again, his wrist plucking the air.
clumsy as i am, the ball finds its way into my hands, warm

as an apology. i stumble forward, inelegant, lacking proper
footwear and disposition. i'm no good at entering.

but i do what i must. his sweaty matted head. the shirt
stained through with a laborious give. i leap as an act

of faith, failing honestly. and then he is showing me
the correct form to take, hands in front, never passing

behind the shoulder. and it is here that i spoil it, a joke about
"faggots," my urge to throw back the wrist

as far as it will go, as if my body were its own sport,
my own foolproof maneuver. as a means to rebuild

the moment, i attempt a faulty replication. the ball smacks
the rim and stumbles off, embarrassed. then we sit

in the grass and i clump blades into a useless death orb.
i am not yet thinking of my coming departure upstate,

or his own across the country, or how years will pass before
a reunion presents itself. we talk about cher,

about the phrase "queer-coded." about those who exists
solely for us to regret. talking shit. talking to continue

with the other. and then the day is done.
we trudge towards the station that will pull me back into

my life, into the many boxes in my living room
full of clothes i don't wear and books i won't read. i know

it's the ego who says i'm a fool to feel hurt. but when
i bring myself to look at him, and embrace as friends do,

a string snaps from the neck of my instrument. *good god,*
it whines. i know. but sometimes there is love

i don't have language for. sometimes all that is left from a day's
good work is the repeating fear of having said

too much, of drawing out the same joke to a point where the mouth
won't give.

i amble down to the platform and stand near the vermin
on the tracks below, not yet in a daze, not yet pitifully

inebriated by sorrow, but swelling nonetheless,
a slow-building tremor reverberating at some hardened

core, as whales do when beached, biding their time before
detonating noxiously. on the platform, a mother says *stop*

to a daughter clutching the fringe of her sundress.
the command unfolds in echo, pulling me towards it until

both of us are vanished in the tunnel.   *stop. stop it.*

tranz

an erasure of *The Transsexual Empire* by Janice Raymond

*

there are many people
with material

sources,
some   i have known   since i began.

the first u.s medical institution

to perform transsexual surgery
        found there was no
surgery
to cure
          the public

my own demise

trans
into the
traumatic
                      the genuine erotic
the money
 institutions

the critical rush

i submit
as a way out of

gender   in fact,
the pursuit of

                                        image
has less to offer
than the flesh.

behind this construction

is   the model
a host of disease

does desire qualify as
a condition requiring psychiatric and medical intervention—

is gender dissatisfaction
the true sex.

i   see it now,
what gender is

k

the caricature   about man-made femininity
the biological essentialism

the theorizing the existence of

identity
my willingness to
               destroy.

i assert there is something
surgery cannot change
it is   history

the body
a raging doubt

things are not so simple
after all is said and done, the transsexual is

really   full-blown genre.

the dissonances
fragment and reconstitute
the heart of the project.

i speak against   sophistication.
even a footnote is royalist behavior.

bodies think little of mutilating
i accept that

trans have suffered
i don't desire
the instrumentality of

woman or man

                      or

the constraints of   who
is real

when i possess
women
what diminishes.

a cavity between   trans and
                       human

lesson

tranz taught me
there is no cruelty which is
impossible

but what i want
for whoever says
i won't have it: a life.

my sister is alive.
my brothers are
alive. my parents,

alive. for them,
i count the yolks
of each broken

year in a bowl. i am
still struggling to remain
someone

any someone
can see. spirit
untethered.

with history i have:
a birth, chasm,

belief in

a romance of hurt.

sometimes
when i am named
inhuman

i like
to imagine the outline
of a child inside me.

not the want
but the wanting
of the want,

the ugly
choice of it. my small
desperate face

repeating.
hello.
hello.

Acknowledgments

Thank you to the editors and journals who published several of these poems in their early forms: *ANMLY, Always Crashing, Brink, Foglifter,* The Academy of American Poets website: poets.org, *Pleiades, The West Review.*

Big, slobbery thank you to Fran Hoepfner and Sydney Choi, and to my frappé girlies Weston Richey and Paige Morris.

Thank you to my iconic poetry pals at Rutgers University-Newark's MFA program for literal edits, advice, and unwavering support even when I was annoying: Sara Munjack, Walter Ancarrow, Fiona Chamness, Evan Cutts, Ricardo Hernandez, Lark Omura, Ana Portnoy-Brimmer, Emily Lee Luan, Nhu Xuân Nguyễn, Diana Li, Ananda Lima, Emily Caris, Catalina Adragna, Charlotte Lindsay, and Caroline Harvey.

Thank you to my fiction friends whose work ethic I find inspiring and terrifying (writing more than one page for workshop): Matthew Broderick, Ali Castleman, Paige Morris, Colin Cage, Aidan Angle, Joshua Irwin, Simeon Marsalis, Ryan Lee Wong, Lauren Parrott, Chester Dubov, Ben Goldstein, Ben Selesnik, and John Blahnik.

Thank you to Rutgers-Newark MFA faculty
Brenda Shaughnessy, Cathy Park Hong, Rigoberto González,
Alice Elliott Dark, and Jim Goodman.

Thank you to my wonderful poet friends on the internet and
offline. Without your guidance, this manuscript would have
been promptly recycled: Zefyr Lisowski, S. Brook Corfman,
torrin a. greathouse, Hannah Bonner, Natalie Eilbert,
Julianne Neely, Aidan Ryan, Alicia Mountain,
Rachelle Toarmino, and Sarah Sgro.

Thank you to Martha Rhodes's manuscript workshop, which
was instrumental in shaping this collection: Sara Munjack,
Kimberly Nunes, Catherine Hoyser, Maria Nazos,
Sam Perkins, Cathy Palermo, Sarah Koken, and Lisa Shapiro.

Thank you to my Pigeon Pages champions: Alisson Wood,
Jiordan Castle, Madeline Mori, Ashley Lopez, Hannah Bae,
Hannah Hirsh, Kat Rejsek, and Amanda Buckley.

Thank you to Chase Berggrun, Kayleb Rae Candrilli, and
Cyrée Jarelle Johnson for blurbs that made me cry and shake.

Thank you to Amber Dermont and Robyn Schiff, my earliest
readers, and teachers.

Thank you to Martha Rhodes, Hannah Matheson, Ryan Murphy, and Trish Marshall for taking this project on with such care and insight.

Finally, thank you mom and dad for accepting early on that I'll never be able to succeed in math or science.

About the Author

Spencer Williams is a trans writer from Chula Vista, California. She is the author of the chapbook *Alien Pink* (The Atlas Review, 2017) and her work has been featured in *Literary Hub, Indiewire,* and *Polygon,* among others. She received her MFA in creative writing from Rutgers University-Newark, and is currently a PhD student in poetics at SUNY, Buffalo.

WE ARE ALSO GRATEFUL TO THOSE INDIVIDUALS WHO PARTICIPATED IN OUR
BUILD A BOOK PROGRAM. THEY ARE:

Anonymous (14), Robert Abrams, Debra Allbery, Nancy Allen,
Michael Ansara, Kathy Aponick, Jean Ball, Sally Ball, Jill Bialosky,
Sophie Cabot Black, Laurel Blossom, Tommye Blount,
Karen and David Blumenthal, Jonathan Blunk, Lee Briccetti,
Jane Martha Brox, Mary Lou Buschi, Anthony Cappo, Carla and
Steven Carlson, Robin Rosen Chang, Liza Charlesworth,
Peter Coyote, Elinor Cramer, Kwame Dawes,
Michael Anna de Armas, Brian Komei Dempster, Renko and
Stuart Dempster, Matthew DeNichilo, Rosalynde Vas Dias,
Patrick Donnelly, Charles R. Douthat, Lynn Emanuel, Blas Falconer,
Laura Fjeld, Carolyn Forché, Helen Fremont and Donna Thagard,
Debra Gitterman, Dorothy Tapper Goldman, Alison Granucci,
Elizabeth T. Gray Jr., Naomi Guttman and Jonathan Meade,
Jeffrey Harrison, KT Herr, Carlie Hoffman, Melissa Hotchkiss,
Thomas and Autumn Howard, Catherine Hoyser, Elizabeth Jackson,
Linda Susan Jackson, Jessica Jacobs, Deborah Jonas-Walsh,
Jennifer Just, Voki Kalfayan, Maeve Kinkead, Victoria Korth,
David Lee and Jamila Trindle, Rodney Terich Leonard, Howard Levy,
Owen Lewis and Susan Ennis, Eve Linn, Matthew Lippman,
Ralph and Mary Ann Lowen, Maja Lukic, Neal Lulofs,
Anthony Lyons, Ricardo Alberto Maldonado, Trish Marshall,
Donna Masini, Deborah McAlister, Carol Moldaw, Michael and
Nancy Murphy, Kimberly Nunes, Matthew Olzmann and
Vivee Francis, Veronica Patterson, Patrick Phillips, Robert Pinsky,
Megan Pinto, Kevin Prufer, Anna Duke Reach, Paula Rhodes,
Yoana Setzer, James Shalek, Soraya Shalforoosh, Peggy Shinner,
Joan Silber, Jane Simon, Debra Spark, Donna Spruijt-Metz,
Arlene Stang, Page Hill Starzinger, Catherine Stearns,
Yerra Sugarman, Arthur Sze, Laurence Tancredi, Marjorie and
Lew Tesser, Peter Turchi, Connie Voisine, Susan Walton,
Martha Webster and Robert Fuentes, Calvin Wei, Allison Benis
White, Lauren Yaffe, and Rolf Yngve.